TRACING NONCONFORMIST ANCELS

Public Record Office
Pocket Guides to Family History

Getting Started in Family History

Using Birth, Marriage and Death Records

Using Census Returns

Using Wills

Using Army Records

Using Navy Records

Tracing Irish Ancestors

Tracing Scottish Ancestors

Using Poor Law Records

Tracing Catholic Ancestors

Tracing Nonconformist Ancestors

TRACING
NONCONFORMIST
ANCESTORS

Michael Gandy

PUBLIC RECORD OFFICE

Public Record Office
Richmond
Surrey
TW9 4DU

ISBN 1 903365 06 6

A catalogue card for this book
is available from the British Library

Front cover: Mrs Horton and Miss Parker,
Primitive Methodist Evangelists
Photograph by Charles Green of Great Yarmouth
Registered by him for copyright 9 November 1887
(COPY 1/382)

Printed by Cromwell Press, Trowbridge, Wiltshire

CONTENTS

INTRODUCTION

This Pocket Guide aims to cover the records of Protestant nonconformists that a family historian will find most useful. After a short historical background, the first part looks at the types of record that are common to most non-conformists, while the second part looks at the specialist records of the main nonconformist groups (with notes on their history). The third part looks at the Anglican and state records as they particularly relate to nonconformists.

Most of the Anglican and state records lump nonconformists together as a group (and do not even distinguish them from Catholics – for whom see the PRO Pocket Guide *Tracing Catholic Ancestors*). The nonconformists' records of themselves vary – depending on their different views of religious practice and authority – but they also have much in common.

This Pocket Guide is about England. Most of it will apply to Welsh records, although the history of Welsh religious denominations is rather different. Scotland and Ireland are separate cultures with separate record systems. Presbyterianism has been very important in both countries, but Scottish and Irish Presbyterianism is *not* an offshoot of English Presbyterianism.

In the period after 1837 the main records for building the family tree are those of the state (civil registration of births, marriages and deaths, census, wills, etc.). It is assumed that the reader is familiar with the state records for tracing English and Welsh ancestry, and this Pocket Guide refers only to records that are concerned with the religious aspect. If you are new to family history, you are advised to read some of the other Pocket Guides in this series, particularly *Getting Started in Family History*, *Using Birth, Marriage and Death Records*, *Using Census Returns* and *Using Wills*. Religious registers can provide very useful supplementary information to that gleaned from state sources. The number of records kept by chapels increased substantially as the 19th century progressed. However, many of these records, such as chapel magazines and photographs of Sunday School outings, are fascinating for understanding people's lives but do not necessarily help in constructing the family tree.

As with all family history research, begin at home by collecting as much information as possible from family relics such as documents, photographs, prayer books and Bibles. Just as important is talking to relatives to gather information, especially names, places and dates. Anecdotes are also useful and help you to build a fuller picture of your family's past. Be sure to record information as you go along: it is a valuable starting point for archival research.

Nonconformists were a literate group who were very committed to their religion. They were mostly property-holders and traders. It is sometimes difficult to find the basic evidence of birth, marriage and death but it is almost always possible to trace them through the wealth of other records in which they appear.

Historical background

Ever since the foundation of the Church of England (Anglicanism) in the 16th century, some Protestants have objected to the concept of a state church. Some, such as the Presbyterians, believed in a strong independent church authority while others, such as the Quakers, did not believe in any religious authority at all. All of them, however, rejected the pyramid of authority with the king at the top. Most of them also believed that the Anglican reforms had not gone far enough and that the Church of England still needed to be purified of 'popish' (Catholic) errors, which is why they were called Puritans.

Between 1558 and 1642 Puritans remained members of the Church of England and tried to change it from the inside. The exceptions were very small groups of Baptists, and the foreign Protestant churches who had permission to have their own ministers and services in their own language. A small number of Puritans chose to go to Holland and a much larger number, led by the Pilgrim Fathers in 1620, chose to settle in New England, USA. Perhaps as many as 20,000 people left England for America in the years 1620–42.

During the Civil War and Commonwealth period (1642–60) the power of the Church of England was destroyed, but the various other groups were unable to take effective control themselves and the consequence was religious anarchy. In that period many Anglicans left England for Virginia because they did not like the Puritan way of doing things.

Between 1660 and 1688 people who did not agree with Anglicanism were persecuted and forced outside the Anglican church. From this point, they were usually called dissenters (in the 18th century) or nonconformists (in the 19th century).

After the Glorious Revolution of 1688 dissenters had to accept exclusion from power as the price of toleration; from now on the gentry were Anglican. This situation continued throughout the 18th century. At first the numbers of dissenters declined, but then they revived under the influence of first John Wesley and then the Evangelicals.

During the 19th century nonconformists increased dramatically in influence and confidence. They now had a great deal in common with many Anglicans and were the powerhouse behind the new 'Victorian morality'. Most nonconformists agreed on the following points:

- **The importance of the Bible** and the individual's responsibility to read it.

- **The 'priesthood of all believers'**, a phrase which reminded them of the basic spiritual equality of all men (not necessarily women). This was strengthened by the fact that nonconformists were very much from one social level – the small farmers and independent tradesmen.

- **The importance of the sermon**. Nonconformists did not believe in priests and an altar, but in ministers and a pulpit.

- **The drawing apart of the gathered community**. Nonconformists believed that most people were never going to be 'born again', and that they should remain aloof from mainstream society.

- **The godly life**. Nonconformists did not believe in salvation by 'works'. Some believed that salvation was available to all (Arminianism) and others that salvation was available only to the 'elect' whom God had chosen (Calvinism), but they all believed that people who were saved would show this by what they did. Any form of bad behaviour threw doubt on this; to them there was no such thing as a bad Christian. (Nonconformists used the word Christian to mean their sort of Christian.)

Fortunately for the family historian, nonconformists never tired of witnessing to the actions of God in their lives, especially their conversion experience. Tens of thousands of spiritual biographies must have appeared in print over the centuries, e.g. in church and missionary magazines and in personal letters. Unfortunately there is no systematic way of finding them.

ARCHIVES AND OTHER SOURCES

Public Record Office (PRO)

The majority of records discussed in this Pocket Guide can be found in the Public Record Office, the national repository for government records in the UK. It holds a wealth of records available for research. There is also an extensive library, with a unique collection of books and periodicals on family history as well as other aspects of history.

▼ **Public Record Office**
Kew
Richmond
Surrey TW9 4DU
General telephone: 020 8876 3444
Telephone number for enquiries and advance document orders: 020 8392 5200
Internet: http://www.pro.gov.uk/

Opening times (closed Sundays and Bank Holidays, and the Saturday of Bank Holiday weekends):

Monday	9 a.m. to 5 p.m.
Tuesday	10 a.m. to 7 p.m.
Wednesday	9 a.m. to 5 p.m.
Thursday	9 a.m. to 7 p.m.
Friday	9 a.m. to 5 p.m.
Saturday	9.30 a.m. to 5 p.m.

No appointment is needed to visit the PRO in Kew, but you will need a reader's ticket to gain access to the research areas. To obtain a ticket, take with you a full UK driving licence or a UK banker's card or a passport if you are a British citizen, and your passport or national identity card if you are not. Note that the last time for ordering documents is 4 p.m. on Mondays, Wednesdays and Fridays; 4.30 p.m. on Tuesdays and Thursdays; and 2.30 p.m. on Saturdays.

Family Records Centre (FRC)

The Family Records Centre is a service for family historians, set up in 1997 by the Office for National Statistics (ONS) and the Public Record Office. It gathers together a range of resources and research facilities specifically designed with family historians in mind, and holds microfilm of many nonconformist registers (1567–1837). Other major holdings include:

- births, marriages and deaths in England and Wales since 1 July 1837

- census returns 1841–1891

- death duty registers 1796–1858, indexes 1796–1858

- wills and administrations of the Prerogative Court of Canterbury 1383–1858

▼ Family Records Centre

1 Myddelton Street
London EC1R 1UW
General telephone: 020 8392 5300
Telephone for birth, marriage and death certificates:
0151 471 4800
Fax: 020 8392 5307
Internet: http://www.pro.gov.uk/
ONS website: http://www.ons.gov.uk/

Opening times (closed Sundays and Bank Holidays):

Monday	9 a.m. to 5 p.m.
Tuesday	10 a.m. to 7 p.m.
Wednesday	9 a.m. to 5 p.m.
Thursday	9 a.m. to 7 p.m.
Friday	9 a.m. to 5 p.m.
Saturday	9.30 a.m. to 5 p.m.

You can visit the FRC in person without an appointment
at the opening times shown.

Society of Genealogists (SoG)

The Society of Genealogists has the best general genealogical collection in the United Kingdom. Almost all published transcripts of material relating to nonconformist
family history will be found there, as well as many other
sources in which nonconformists appear incidentally.

▼ **Society of Genealogists (SoG)**
14 Charterhouse Buildings
Goswell Road
London EC1M 7BA
Telephone: 020 7251 8799
Internet: http://www.sog.org.uk/

Opening times (closed Sundays and Mondays):

Tuesday	10 a.m. to 6 p.m.
Wednesday	10 a.m. to 8 p.m.
Thursday	10 a.m. to 8 p.m.
Friday	10 a.m. to 6 p.m.
Saturday	10 a.m. to 6 p.m.

You do not have to be a member of the Society of Genealogists to use its library, although you do have to pay a fee. You can visit it without an appointment. It is conveniently located for you to combine a trip there with a trip to the FRC.

Specialist libraries and archives

The most vital early source on nonconformists, the records of quarter sessions (see p. 53), are usually found in local record offices. All the major denominations maintain an archive, but these usually concentrate on the national records of the denomination, its political role and its theological history. It has been the policy for many years to encourage the deposit of individual chapel records in the local record office, and enquiries should be made there first.

A great deal of work has been done on Puritan and non-conformist clergy, and the best library nationally for the sources is Dr Williams's Library. This library specializes in religious history; it is excellent on denominational history and the histories of congregations and the lives and publications of anybody prominent. It does not hold any specifically genealogical material.

▼ **Dr Williams's Library**
14 Gordon Square
London WC1H 0AG
Email: 101340.2541@compuserve.com

For the personal, estate or business papers of families, it is always worth checking the database of the Royal Commission on Historical Manuscripts. They usually have complete catalogues but do not hold any source material.

▼ **Royal Commission on Historical Manuscripts**
Quality House
Quality Court
Chancery Lane
London WC2A 1HP
Telephone: 020 7242 1198
Fax: 020 7831 3550
Email: nra@hmc.gov.uk
http://www.hmc.gov.uk/

Printed material, for example autobiographies or religious tracts, may be in the British Library.

PART ONE: RECORDS
COMMON TO NONCONFORMISTS

Nonconformist registers

Many nonconformist congregations kept registers of births or baptisms, and deaths or burials. (Marriages of non-conformists (excepting Quakers) between 1754 and 1837 took place in the Anglican church – and probably many of the nonconformist marriages before 1754.) Family historians start with the great convenience that a very high proportion of the known registers to June 1837 were handed in to public keeping by 1857, and are in the PRO, Kew, in series RG 4, RG 5, RG 6 and RG 8. They can be seen on microfilm at Kew and at the FRC (see pp. 13–14), except RG 6 which will be available at these sites from 2001. They are officially called non-parochial registers.

The nonconformists had campaigned for this handover and cooperated with the commission inspecting their registers. Once their records were 'authenticated' and in public keeping they could be used as legal evidence, particularly of age and legitimacy, in the same way as Anglican records.

- **Series RG 4** contains 4,680 volumes of registers that were authenticated in this way. Apart from the registers of individual congregations, it includes the indexes to the registers of Dr Williams's Library and the Wesleyan Methodist Metropolitan Registry (see p. 24). This series also contains the registers of Bunhill Fields, an important nonconformist cemetery in London.

- **Series RG 5** contains the original certificates relating to Dr Williams's Library and the Wesleyan Methodist Metropolitan Registry.

- **Series RG 6** contains the registers of the Quakers (Religious Society of Friends).

- **Series RG 8** contains 314 volumes of non-Anglican registers that were not authenticated because they were handed in too late. They are not considered to be any less reliable for family history purposes. They also include the registers of the Lying-In Hospital in Endell Street, Holborn, and the burial registers of Victoria Park Cemetery 1853–76, important London sources that are neither Anglican nor nonconformist.

(Series RG 7 contains a number of Anglican registers not relating to parishes – for example, the Fleet Registers and the registers of Greenwich Hospital. These are important sources, particularly for London families, but they are not nonconformist.)

The registers in RG 4 and RG 8 were microfilmed many years ago and can be seen at the Family Records Centre and at Kew. The registers are widely available elsewhere (e.g. in local record offices and at the SoG), and many have been transcribed. Basic information from many of these registers is included in the *International Genealogical Index (IGI)*, but not the details of deaths or burials. Details of many of the certificates from Dr Williams's Library and the Wesleyan Methodist Metropolitan Registry are included on the recent British Isles Vital Records Index. So, all in all, this material is very accessible and, up to a point, researchers check it every time they look at the *IGI*.

However, there are a couple of points to watch out for:

- Many religious congregations did not keep baptism, marriage and burial records like the ones family historians are accustomed to finding in the Church of England parish registers. Many of them did not baptize children (some of them did not baptize anybody). Others did not believe that marriage was a religious act. Many of them did not believe that burial was a religious act either. However, it is not safe to assume that the event did not take place if you cannot locate the record.

- The majority of the deposited registers relate to Methodists and date from later than 1780. A high proportion of the other registers date from 1750 or later, yet many nonconformist congregations claim a foundation date of around 1662 or 1689. Were there earlier records which have been lost? The answer in many cases is that there probably were – but we shall never know.

Baptisms

It has already been pointed out that until the Civil War almost all the groups who were against the Church of England were *inside* it. Their baptisms, marriages and burials are all in the parish registers and we know of their Puritan beliefs from other sources.

During the Civil War the system of parishes and parish registers was seriously weakened. Many people ceased coming to church and after the restoration of the monarchy in 1660 never really came back. The baptisms of their children (if they were baptized) did not take place in the parish church and are not recorded in the parish register. Thus many children were born for whom there is no known record of birth or baptism now, and perhaps never was, except in their father's pocket-book, Bible or diary, or on a sampler they embroidered as a child. This can be a problem for the family historian.

Marriages

Many nonconformists were against church marriage in principle. However, legal marriage was the only protection of a wife's and children's inheritance. If there was no church marriage then the man's next heir would be his brother or nephew, and the wife and children would have no standing.

Until 1753 marriages other than in the parish church were legally recognized – irregular but not invalid. However, in practice most nonconformists except Quakers went to the Anglican church for their marriage.

In 1753 Lord Hardwicke's Marriage Act finally defined legal marriage as one which took place in the Church of England. Only Quakers and Jews were exempted from that requirement, and if a non-Anglican congregation was performing marriages before that date (Huguenots certainly were), they stopped. All marriages of nonconformists excepting Quakers between 1754 and 1837 took place in the Church of England.

It seems probable that a high proportion of nonconformist marriages before 1754 also took place in church, often by marriage licence. If the marriage did not take place in church, we are unlikely to find a record of it. Only two Presbyterian chapels are known to have marriage registers deposited in the PRO: Stockton-on-Tees (1688–1720) and Whitby (1695–1710).

Register offices were established in 1837 because the older types of nonconformist wanted them. A 19th century marriage in a register office does *not* imply indifference or atheism.

Burials

Objections to Anglican burial of nonconformists might come from either side. Nonconformists disagreed with the concept of consecrated ground, but the church cemetery was usually the only place in the parish where anyone had ever been buried.

Quite often a nonconformist congregation was led to establish a burying ground of its own by the refusal of the Anglican minister to bury one of their members (usually for lack of baptism). However, England, unlike America, never developed the custom of family burial grounds.

The deposited burial registers in RG 4 almost always start at a later date than the baptisms, and often long after. It is not known whether earlier burials have not been recorded – or took place in the Anglican churchyard, and are therefore hopefully recorded in the parish register.

Are they really the registers of another congregation?

A further warning. The registers are catalogued under the name of the congregation whose minister deposited them. They were the registers of that congregation when they were deposited – but had they always been? Many congregations were not concerned with keeping registers, and the earliest notebook may have been a personal register of the minister, which travelled with him when he moved to a new congregation.

Some advantages of the registers

- There were no rules about how nonconformist registers should be compiled, and some ministers used a printed form which recorded not only the birth and baptism dates and the name of the father and mother, but the name of the maternal grandfather as well. This helps enormously in recognizing the correct entry of marriage in an Anglican register. Some of the registers also contain other material, such as membership lists and disciplinary material.

- Some of the nonconformist registers are very large. This particularly applies to some of the burial registers. It has long been recognized by family historians that Bunhill Fields buried a very high percentage of the nonconformists in London; Spa Fields in Clerkenwell is less well known, but the burial registers run to tens of thousands.

As well as the records of individual congregations, there are two very important series of registers in series RG 4 and RG 5:

The register of Dr Williams's Library

In 1742 a committee of nonconformists, the Protestant Dissenting Deputies, arranged with Dr Williams's Library, the most important library for nonconformist studies, to set up a register of births. This was to give the name of the child, the date and place of birth, and the names of the parents, duly certified by reliable witnesses. The register took a while to establish itself, but from 1759 there is a steadily increasing number of entries. Many are in family groups and date from long after the births they record. For the years 1742 to 1837, there are 29,865 entries.

The Wesleyan Methodist Metropolitan Registry

The records of the Wesleyan Methodist Metropolitan Registry (1818–37), based in Paternoster Row, near St Paul's Cathedral in the City of London, follow similar lines to those of Dr Williams's Library, and record the births and baptisms of 10,291 children.

Other records

Most nonconformist congregations made a distinction between members and attenders. Ministers and elders took responsibility for church discipline and investigated questions of bad behaviour, business practice and freedom to marry. Additionally, they were often very active in helping members who were in difficulties.

Disciplinary records survive occasionally from Baptist and Congregational congregations, and more frequently from Huguenot congregations and Quaker meetings. Most Presbyterian, Baptist and Congregationalist congregations had the same sort of systems for church discipline and pastoral oversight as Quakers and Huguenots, but comparatively few of their minute books have survived.

Books, newspapers and periodicals

Nonconformists were literate and usually prosperous people who considered religion to be very important. Many of them were deeply involved in political battles or in public campaigns on moral issues. Others regularly wrote and preached, aiming to convert people to Christianity. Many of their books, pamphlets and sermons contain details from their own lives or anecdotes about named individuals.

In the 19th century religious newspapers flourished. The following were the most important:

The Nonconformist (1841)
The Friend (1843)
The Freeman which became
  The Baptist Times and Freeman (1853)
The Christian World (1859)
The Methodist Recorder (1861)
The Primitive Methodist (1870)
The War Cry (1880)

There were many others, as well as smaller magazines publicizing the work of particular societies or missions. Although some were aimed at particular denominations, most had a broadly low-church evangelical view which was acceptable to a wide range of churchgoers.

ⓘ **Remember**

Nonconformists appear in all the normal state records and in all the records that are not concerned with religion. Their marriages and burials may well be recorded in the Church of England parish registers. However, many of them did not baptize children.

Nonconformists' own registers were handed into the PRO by 1857, but there were many chapels that did not keep the sort of records family historians want, or whose records have not survived.

PART TWO:
THE MAIN DENOMINATIONS

All of the main denominations have a distinctive style and particular points of belief or practice that they emphasize.

Many older congregations still have their own records; others may be in the denominational archives or in the local record office or equivalent (see also p. 16). For many independent congregations that close there may be no successor body and the records may remain with the last minister, the church secretary or one of the deacons or elders. A great deal of useful material is in private hands.

The Public Record Office has no archives of individual congregations apart from the non-parochial registers to 1837 (some to 1857).

Baptists

These were also sometimes called Anabaptists, but this word had negative connotations and on the whole Baptists did not use it themselves. The chief point about Baptists is that they do not believe in the baptism of children. This can be a problem for the family historian researching the 17th and 18th centuries, but by the early 19th century many Baptist congregations had begun to keep a register of births. From 1837 there should be a birth certificate under state registration.

The early Baptist congregations were all independent and might hold any of a range of Puritan beliefs. There were two early groupings. One drew its inspiration from John Smyth, who had taken a group of Baptists to Amsterdam during the reign of Elizabeth I when persecution in England became severe, and Thomas Helwys, who brought them back in 1611 when the situation improved. They believed in general salvation (Arminianism) and were thus known as General Baptists. The second group dates its foundation to 1633; they believed in the Calvinist doctrine of election and were often known as Particular Baptists.

A third group would allow communion only to those they had accepted into membership; they were known as Strict Baptists. Some groups were known as Strict and Particular Baptists – which was just a clear statement of their doctrine to other Christians who would know the special meaning of those words.

The first Baptist church in Wales was founded in 1649 at Ilston, near Swansea, and there were Baptists amongst the Cromwellian soldiers who settled in Ireland in the 1650s. A General Baptist Assembly in England was formed in 1653. However, there were very few Baptists in Scotland until the late 18th century.

There were about 58,000 Baptists in 1700. Numbers declined in the 18th century but revived towards the end of the century under the influence of Methodism. The General Baptists' 'New Connexion', a loose grouping, was formed in 1770, and those who did not associate with that mostly drifted towards Unitarianism (see p. 45). The Particular Baptists were brought together and revived by the foundation of the Baptist Missionary Society in 1792. This gave them a new focus, and the first Baptist Union of Particular Baptists was founded in 1813. General Baptists and Particular Baptists united in 1891. However, each congregation remains fundamentally independent and there is no standard theological position or form of service, although, as with all nonconformists except Quakers, the sermon tends to be central.

Further reading: G. R. Breed, *My Ancestors were Baptists* (see p. 63); publications of the Baptist Historical Society.

Congregationalists/Independents

Congregationalists, otherwise known as Independents and sometimes just as Separatists, were not founded by any one person and did not form a church; however, they looked back to the example of Robert Browne, who founded a Separatist church in Norwich in the 16th century. They believed in the freewill association of the godly into groups which appointed a minister. There was no higher or overseeing body; every congregation was independent and run by deacons or elders appointed by the congregation.

There was no particular theological viewpoint. The service was a balance between the minister's and the congregation's beliefs. If the congregation as a whole were not happy, they would expect the minister to take account of their views. If individuals were not happy, they looked for a minister whose teaching they preferred.

In the 17th and 18th centuries the words 'Independent' and 'Congregational' were more or less interchangeable. Moreover many Presbyterian churches were described as 'independent' simply because they were independent of the Church of England. In 1700 there were about 59,000 Congregationalists; numbers declined until the mid-18th century and then slowly rose again. In the 19th century Congregationalists developed as a more defined denomination, although still a voluntary association of independent churches; the word independent came to mean 'standing aloof from any formal associations', as in the more modern Federation of Independent Evangelical Churches.

Further reading: D. J. H. Clifford, *My Ancestors were Congregationalists* (see p. 64).

Huguenots

Huguenots were French Protestants. About 60,000 came to England in around 1685, when Protestantism was suppressed in France by the Revocation of the Edict of Nantes. About 40,000 settled in London; the others almost all went to towns in the south-east of England. A few went to the west country, particularly Bristol, Plymouth and Stonehouse. There were no settlements in the Midlands, the north, Wales or Scotland (although descendants of the original immigrants may have moved there later).

Huguenots were of all social levels. In London those of the upper class, and those who worked in the luxury trades, settled in Soho and nearby parishes in Westminster. Many of the poorer Huguenots were weavers and settled in Spitalfields and Bethnal Green in east London. Both groups intermarried with English families. Many of them became members of the Church of England, but others joined English nonconformist churches.

The Huguenots were Calvinists and their church government was in the style of the Presbyterians. They were basically welcomed and there are extensive records of the charity they received (the 'King's Bounty'), all now indexed at the Huguenot Library.

▼ **Huguenot Library**
   University College
   Gower Street
   London WC1E 6BT
   Telephone: 020 7380 7094
   Email: s.massil@ucl.ac.uk

The most important French church in London was in Threadneedle Street, in the City (the registers have been published by the Huguenot Society), and most refugees presented themselves there first. If possible they gave a character reference, as many English nonconformists did on moving to a new congregation. If they were not in good standing, they made public repentance and were admitted to membership. Either way, the records are usually in family groups and say where in France the people came from.

Within a few years after 1685, more than a dozen new French churches had opened in London to cater for the influx. All the known records are in the PRO; they have been published by the Huguenot Society and the basic information is on the *IGI*. These churches flourished as long as their members wanted services in French, but numbers declined and all the London churches have now closed except the lineal descendant of Threadneedle Street, which is in Soho Square.

All the French churches have registers of baptisms and marriage. The records are in French but are fairly easy to interpret, and they give more information than many English records. The baptism registers often give the date of birth, the mother's maiden name and the names of two godparents (who are often relatives). Marriage registers often state where the bride and groom were born and give the names of their fathers and mothers.

The French churches did not have any burial grounds of their own. Huguenots were usually buried in the Anglican churchyard and appear in the parish registers. In London they may be buried in the nonconformist cemetery of Bunhill Fields.

Many Huguenots appear in the naturalization records in the PRO (series HO 1). These have been published by the Huguenot Society for the years 1509–1800.

Huguenots established a number of charities to look after their own poor, and the records of some of these have been published by the Huguenot Society, either in their record series (known as the Quarto Series) or in their annual *Proceedings*. A great deal of other material, much of it concerned with charity, is unpublished but has been microfilmed and is available at the Huguenot Library.

Although Huguenots were strictly French, the word is often used to describe an earlier group of refugees who came from the Spanish Netherlands (now Belgium and Holland) in 1567, when the Duke of Alva was sent by King Philip of Spain to suppress Protestants by force. They settled in the same south-eastern towns – London, Canterbury, Dover, Sandwich, Southampton, Colchester, Ipswich and Norwich – and there are records of them in the Anglican parish registers or in the registers of their own chapels. All known registers have been published by the Huguenot Society of Great Britain and Ireland, and the originals are in the PRO in series RG 4. This group can be recognized in the lay subsidy records at the PRO (series E 179) because they were foreigners and therefore paid double the tax.

Further reading: R. D. Gwynn, *Huguenot Heritage: The History and Contribution of the Huguenots in Britain* (see p. 64); Huguenot Society Publications (Quarto Series; *Proceedings* and *Huguenot Families*). For Ireland, see G. L. Lee, *The Huguenot Settlements in Ireland* (Longmans, Green, 1936).

Independents/Separatists

See Congregationalists (p. 29).

Methodists

Methodism is numerically by far the most important branch of nonconformity. Yet theologically it is not non-conformist at all and has nothing to distinguish it from evangelical Anglicanism. Methodists believe in sacraments, ordain ministers and use the Anglican prayer books. One peculiarity of Methodist organization is the circuit, whereby ministers preach in different places each week. Another is the requirement that ministers move frequently.

The Methodists were not established as a separate church until the 1780s, but many Methodist registers are held at the PRO in series RG 4 and 8 (see p. 18) and their chapels are listed in the register of places of worship in RG 31.

Methodism arose in the mid-18th century from the preaching of John Wesley, George Whitefield and, in Wales, Howell Harris – who all, however, differed on important points. Their aim was to revive the Church of England, to persuade churchgoers to live their religion rather than just attend services. This was seen as very exciting and refreshing by many; and as dangerous, emotional and uncontrollable by others.

John Wesley's followers eventually parted company with the Church of England and founded a separate church. For many years after that, however, there was no antagonism between the two and many Methodists attended evangelical Anglican services as well as their own.

John Wesley was an Arminian (believing that salvation is available to all). George Whitefield was a Calvinist and his followers were therefore known as Calvinistic Methodists. One of his most committed converts was the Countess of Huntingdon, who financed chapels and provided ministers. Some churches were therefore described as Calvinistic Methodist (Countess of Huntingdon's Connexion) but they did not differ religiously from standard Calvinistic Methodism.

Calvinistic Methodism was very successful in Wales, as was nonconformity in general, and by the end of the 19th century perhaps as many as 80 per cent of Welsh churchgoers attended some form of nonconformist chapel.

After the death of Wesley, Methodism began to fragment. The Methodist New Connexion was formed in 1797; the Primitive Methodists (a sort of early Pentecostal) in 1807; the Bible Christians (mostly in the west country) in 1815; the Protestant Methodists in 1827; and the Wesleyan Methodist Association in 1836. Another group of reformers began to agitate in 1849 and eventually formed the United Methodist Free Churches in 1857; others formed the Wesleyan Reform Union.

After so much fracture, the late 19th century saw efforts at union. The United Methodist Church was founded in 1907 and this combined with the Primitive Methodists and the Wesleyan Methodists in 1932. These divisions, which can be confusing for the family historian, all seemed very important to our ancestors!

Methodists have registers of baptism and burial but had no objection to Anglican marriages, and they may have continued to marry in the Anglican Church, even after 1837, until their own chapels were licensed.

Further reading: W. Leary, *My Ancestors were Methodists* (see p. 64).

Moravians

A Moravian mission sent by Count von Zinzendorf first came to England in 1723, but it was the influence of the Moravians whom John Wesley met on his voyage to America in 1735 which explains their importance in the history of English nonconformity. The Moravians had a number of congregations in England and their pre-1837 records are in PRO series RG 4, but their numbers were always fairly small. By the end of the 18th century there were something over 20 congregations with less than 5,000 members, although there were many attendees.

Further reading: The best description of Moravian records for family historians remains D. J. Steel's account in *Sources for Nonconformist Genealogy and Family History* (see p. 64).

Muggletonians

This was another movement which arose from the chaos of the Civil War and Commonwealth. In 1652 John Reeve declared that he and his cousin, Lodowick Muggleton, were the Two Last Witnesses in the Book of Revelation. Reeve died in 1658 and Muggleton became sole leader. Two hundred and forty-eight followers attended his funeral in 1698. Numbers never really grew much further; there are a few lists of names but no genealogically useful records as such.

Further reading: W. Lamont, 'The Muggletonians 1652–1979' (see p. 64). The Muggletonians' archive is in the British Library.

Presbyterians

Presbyterianism was the establishment religion in Scotland, except for a short period in the late 17th century. It therefore does not count as 'nonconformist' in that country.

In England many Puritans held Presbyterian views on church government, but there were no separate churches until the Civil War period. During the Civil War, Parliament was dominated by Presbyterians; and their form of church government was established nationally in 1648. However, they were never able to establish the disciplinary enforcement that was so effective in Scotland. After the Restoration of the Monarchy in 1660, about 2,000 Anglican ministers were 'ejected' and they formed the backbone of nonconformist congregations. Presbyterians were the largest group amongst these, and after a generation of persecution they accepted toleration and exclusion from power, as did the other dissenters.

Very few Presbyterian books of discipline have survived, but their standards and approach may be gauged by looking at Scottish material or at the equivalent books of the Huguenots, in particular *Minutes of the Consistory of the French Church of London, Threadneedle Street, 1679–1692* (Huguenot Society, Quarto Series vol. 58, 1994). The minutes of Quaker meetings also show similarities, although Quakers were more inclined to discuss and persuade.

In 1700 there were estimated to be about 179,000 Presbyterians, but numbers declined throughout the 18th century and this was exacerbated by the drift towards Unitarianism (ceasing to believe in the Trinity). By the end of the 18th century most groups that were still called Presbyterian were actually Unitarian. They remained 'rational' at a time when the pendulum was swinging towards Methodist 'enthusiasm'. In practice English Presbyterianism had declined almost to extinction, and the increasing number of Presbyterian churches built in the 19th century mostly catered for people who had come to England from Scotland and Northern Ireland, where Presbyterianism, despite its internal troubles, continued to flourish.

Further reading: A. Ruston, *My Ancestors were English Presbyterians/Unitarians* (see p. 64).

Quakers
(The Religious Society of Friends; 'Friends' for short)

Quakerism arose in the East Midlands in the late 1640s as a consequence of the religious turmoil of the Civil War period. It spread quickly in the north of England in the early 1650s and in the south from 1654. It rejected formal services, ministers (and the payment of tithes to support them) and church buildings ('steeplehouses'). It stressed the equality of all, and Quakers were frequently punished by magistrates for contempt of court in refusing to take off their hats or pay 'hat-honour', as they described it. In the early years Quakers were perceived as very radical and dangerous, but their commitment to non-violence and their generally respectable nature soon meant that their moral stand was recognized even when they were refusing to comply with the law.

Quakers have a reputation for having kept excellent records. This is deserved, but with some qualification. Many records have not survived, but the survival rate for Quaker records is much higher than for the Baptists, Presbyterians and Independents. Many Quaker groups were founded in the early 1650s, but the formal record-keeping system was not established until 1669. Thus, many groups have excellent records – but not from the beginning.

The Quaker registers of births (not baptisms), marriages and deaths/burials were handed into public keeping with the other nonconformist registers but are in a separate series, RG 6. They are currently being microfilmed and will be available at the Family Records Centre and Kew this year. However, before sending them in, the Friends had them abstracted and calendared by counties, or groups of counties. These indexes, known as digests, are the first port of call for the family historian. They are on microfilm and are available at Friends House Library and at the Society of Genealogists (see p. 15).

▼ **Library of the Society of Friends**
Friends House
Euston Road
London NW1 2BJ
Telephone: 020 7663 1135
Email: library@quaker.org.uk
Internet: http://www.library@quaker.org.uk

In the case of births and deaths/burials, the digests often contain all the information in the original (which should nevertheless be checked). In the case of marriages, Quakers developed the custom of everybody present signing the register as witnesses. Many Quaker marriage records thus include dozens of names of people who were present, which is of course extremely valuable to the genealogist.

Quakers refused to use the pagan names for days and months and always used numbers, e.g. 3rd 6th mo[nth].

Before 1752, however, the New Year began in March, which Quakers therefore numbered as the first month. 3rd 6th mo is thus the 3rd of August, *not June*. Sometimes Quakers used arabic numbers for the day and roman numbers for the month, but it is always useful to look at a series of figures to find numbers over 12 in order to be certain which column is the day and which is the month: if 21.6. is the 21st of August, then 6.7. should be the 6th of September. The Quaker notation 23.xii.1732 means 23rd February 1733!

Quakers developed a system of meetings, with minutes, to record their business. At local level Preparative Meetings drew up material for the Monthly Meetings, of which there were 151 in England and Wales in 1694. In many meetings men and women met separately and divided the work between them: they dealt with finance and property matters; general questions of discipline; the recording of sufferings (persecution); arrangements for apprenticeship; poor relief; membership, including removals to and from the meeting; and the important question of clearness for marriage.

All early nonconformist groups were concerned that young people should not marry without their parents' consent, and they were always concerned to check that neither of the young couple had already promised themselves to someone else. Like most religious groups, Quakers tried to discourage people from marrying outside the group.

The Quaker attitude to discipline was caring and persevering, but in the end if individuals continued their 'disorderly walking' (e.g. missing meetings; excessive drinking; dishonesty in business, or bankruptcy; fornication before marriage; paying tithes; condoning war), they would be disowned. Many Quakers in practice married in church, either under persuasion by a non-Quaker partner or to ensure legality. This was a very serious offence, but disownment did not necessarily stop the culprits from attending the meeting; they were just no longer in good standing. Many rejoined the fold and went on to respectability.

Some of the minutes of local Monthly Meetings are at Friends House Library, but many are in local record offices.

The Monthly Meetings sent representatives to the Quarterly Meetings, which in turn sent representatives to the Yearly Meeting held in London. The records of these committees are at Friends House Library but are of much less genealogical interest.

In their early years Quakers were fairly severely persecuted. They were frequently presented to quarter sessions with other nonconformists, but in their case the proceedings were often stalled by their refusal to swear the standard oaths. They were then often committed for contempt of court, and some Quakers spent many years in prison without ever being convicted.

Since Quakers refused to pay tithes, the standard tax for the support of the Anglican church, many vicars took them to court for the recovery of this normal part of their income. They often appointed bailiffs, and Quaker records are full of references to bailiffs who took goods to a greater value than the tithes refused.

In 1675, the Yearly Meeting established a 'constant meeting about sufferings'. The records, the 'Great Books of Sufferings', document county by county what Quakers had to endure. They are available at Friends House Library and on microfilm; there are contemporary indexes. In 1753, Joseph Besse published a two-volume *Collection of the Sufferings of the People called Quakers for the Testimony of a Good Conscience* (see p. 63). Arranged by county, this covers the years from about 1650 to 1689 and gathers together all the most interesting episodes; it is the next step in Quaker research after the digests of births, marriages and deaths. The six northern counties have recently been republished by William Sessions of York, and others are expected in the near future.

Although Quakers rejected the concept of paid ministers, they soon accepted leadership by elders and overseers – 'seasoned Friends' – who came to be called ministers. On the minister's death, a 'testimony' (i.e. an obituary and appreciation) was frequently sent to the Yearly Meeting. These were published and an indexed list is available for the years 1700 to 1843 at Friends House Library. In fact testimonies of many deceased Friends were published in *Piety Promoted* (1701–1829, eleven parts) and in the

Annual Monitor. There is an index to over 20,000 deaths recorded in the *Annual Monitor* over the years 1813–92 (J. J. Green, 1894)

The 'Dictionary of Quaker Biography' at Friends House library is an ongoing loose-leaf compilation. It is unsystematic, but well worth browsing.

Quakers often established their own burial grounds. However, they disapproved of gravestones, and even modern Quaker stones are always plain and lacking those extra details which family historians find so useful. Friends also disapproved of portraits, and most engravings of early Friends date from later and are created from the imagination.

In 1682 William Penn established the North American colony of Pennsylvania, and about 23,000 Quakers emigrated there over the next 30 years. This weakened Quakers at home, and by the middle of the 18th century numbers had declined drastically. During the years 1650 to 1750 you are very likely to have Quaker ancestry; but after that Quakers became a very small, although very influential, group.

There were quite large numbers of Quakers in Ireland, but comparatively few in Scotland or Wales. For records of early Quakers in America, start with W. W. Hinshaw, *Encyclopaedia of Quaker Genealogy* (7 vols, 1936–70).

Further reading: E. H. Milligan and M. J. Thomas, *My Ancestors were Quakers: How Can I Find Out More about Them?* (see p. 64); *Quaker Connections* (journal of the Quaker Family History Society, 32 Ashburnham Road, Ampthill, Bedfordshire MK45 2RH); *Journal of the Friends Historical Society,* Friends House Library.

Unitarians

Unitarians do not believe in the Trinity. This was not a publicly acceptable position in the 16th and 17th centuries and it carried the death sentence. Unitarians formed no early congregations under that name. As a view, Unitarianism gained acceptance during the 18th century and many Presbyterians, in particular, became Unitarians. There were middle-class 'academies' and some meetings, but Unitarians avoided the law by calling their groups societies: the most important was the Unitarian Society for Promoting Christian Knowledge, founded in 1791. From 1789 Unitarians were in the forefront of support for the French Revolution and were caught in the backlash when it became extreme. They were seen as radicals and revolutionaries; English public opinion turned against them, and for a while there was no question of effective agitation against the laws that made Unitarianism illegal. It was not until the Trinity Act of 1813 that it was legal for a congregation to be described as Unitarians.

Unitarians have always been very few in number.

Further reading: A. Ruston, *My Ancestors were English Presbyterians/Unitarians* (see p. 64).

Other nonconformist groups

- There are a number of small denominations represented amongst the authenticated registers in series RG 4: Inghamites, Irvingites, New Jerusalemites and Swedenborgians.

- The only major Christian denomination to be founded in 19th century-England was the Salvation Army, who have excellent records of their members and of their widespread work for the poor. See R. Wiggins, *My Ancestors were in the Salvation Army* (see p. 64).

- The Church of Jesus Christ of Latter-day Saints (Mormons) gained many converts in the years 1837 to 1850 but always encouraged their members to emigrate to America.

- Many thousands of individual, independent groups have started, flourished for a while, and then closed. All of them have left some record somewhere and played a vital part in the lives of their members.

PART THREE:
ANGLICAN AND STATE RECORDS

Anglican records

Parish registers

Registers of births, marriages and burials were ordered to be kept in every parish in 1538. Not all have survived from the beginning; but where they have, they are the family historian's most important record source.

It has already been stated that almost all Puritans stayed inside the Church of England until the Civil War began in 1642. In the years leading up to 1642 many Puritan ministers had developed their religious positions and, once they had the freedom to do so, preached their doctrines to their congregations. From 1643, people who disagreed with the priest could withdraw. Thus, many Puritans ceased to come to churches where the minister was committed to High Anglican beliefs.

As the war progressed and the Church of England organization fell apart, ministers who died, left or were driven away were not always replaced. Many parish registers were badly kept or not kept at all, and we often cannot find entries for events we feel confident took place *somewhere*. This is particularly true of baptisms.

In 1653 marriage registrars were appointed who were widely acceptable to Puritans, so from then until 1660 most marriages are likely to have been registered.

After 1660 nonconformists withdrew or were ejected from the Church of England. Many of their marriages and most of their burials still took place there and may be recorded, but many nonconformists must have taken their children for baptism to one of their own ministers – and we have very few nonconformist baptism registers dated as early as this. Some groups did not believe in infant baptism at all, and only the Quakers developed the idea of registering births when no religious ceremony was involved.

Entries of burial sometimes note that nonconformists were buried without Anglican ceremonies; local circumstances depended very much on the personal relations between the individuals concerned.

Where individuals had been excommunicated, this is often noted in the register (most such entries are from the 1660s and 1670s).

An Act of 1696 instructed ministers to record the births of nonconformists' children, but it fell into disuse by about 1704. Many entries relating to nonconformists, particularly marriages and burials, appear in the parish registers without comment after toleration was granted in 1691. As already explained, all marriages of nonconformists (except for Quakers) are in the parish registers from

1754 to 1837 (and they did not have second ceremonies, as many of the Catholics did).

Many Methodists were slow to cut themselves off completely from the Anglican church, and continued to be happy with Anglican baptism; everyone was aware that only Anglican registers were legal evidence of the children's date of birth, parentage and legitimacy. In many areas nonconformists continued to be buried in the Anglican churchyard until 1853, when borough cemeteries were established.

Other parish material

Until the New Poor Law of 1834 the Anglican parish was the administrative unit for the collection of local taxes and the administration of poor relief. Nonconformists had no religious objection to paying rates for the poor, or for lighting, paving, sewerage or scavenging, and they appear in rate books without comment. Very few of them were poor enough to need poor relief, but where they did they received it without distinction. Many nonconformists took their turns at the various parish jobs. Most nonconformists also paid tithes until the 19th century, when they began to be commuted for everyone. Only Quakers took a stand on this issue.

In the 18th century people were able to distinguish between the parish as a provider of religion (which the nonconformists didn't want) and as one of the providers of important local services, which had to be paid for.

Monumental inscriptions

Puritans were uneasy about gravestones marking a place of burial but they had no objection to memorial inscriptions, and in the early years Puritan gentry put up the same plaques as their High Church neighbours. By the time the practice of erecting gravestones spread to the middle classes, most nonconformists also put them up. Only the Quakers objected and did not change their view until 1859. Even after that, Quaker grave markers were of the simplest type, giving minimal information.

Marriage licences, wills and administrations

Puritans, dissenters and nonconformists, like everybody else, took out marriage licences and had their wills proved in the Church of England's bishops courts or applied there for letters of administration. Wills often give important clues about nonconformity, especially any instructions about the funeral, and it is worth checking up on any books that are listed in the inventory. Beware of reading Puritan attitudes into the standard preamble, which often talks about being saved 'through the only merits of Jesus Christ' or similar. These words were standard, or may represent the preference of the lawyer who drew up the will.

During the Commonwealth period (1653–60) bishops courts were abolished and all wills were proved in one national court. These records are part of the series of wills proved in the Prerogative Court of Canterbury. Copies of these wills and their indexes can be seen on microfilm at the FRC.

Quakers refused to swear the necessary oaths because they objected to any form of swearing. The other non-conformist groups did not share this view, so any statement that an individual affirmed rather than swore is almost certainly an indication of Quakerism.

Licences for teachers and midwives

From the reign of Queen Elizabeth these two important groups were obliged to be communicant members of the Church of England; this was at first to ensure they were not Catholics, but the rule was applied to nonconformists when they left the Church of England. The rule about licensing midwives died out. By the 18th century non-conformist teachers could set up privately without fear of the church, but parish schoolmasters still had to be Anglicans.

Ecclesiastical court records

Those who were accused of some form of wrong belief will be found in ecclesiastical court records, which are usually in the diocesan record office. But those who simply refused to come to church were cited before quarter sessions, because they were disobeying the law.

Up until the Civil War, ecclesiastical courts remained very powerful. They dealt with accusations of 'heresy', and Puritans who caused trouble would be cited before them. However, there was nothing illegal about the ex-pression of Puritan opinions in the context of preaching, pamphleteering or politics, and most of those cited before the ecclesiastical courts were Anglicans guilty of 'moral crimes', from nagging and wife-beating to adultery and incest. Many couples were cited for 'fornication before marriage'. For a few this may have been a expression of the standard Puritan view that church marriage was wrong and that the binding ceremony was betrothal.

In extreme cases, the ecclesiastical courts might proceed to excommunication.

Ecclesiastical courts were abolished during the Civil War and Commonwealth period and never regained their former power.

Bishops' visitations

From time to time most parishes were required to report on the spiritual state of their congregations, and this included reporting on the number of dissenters and papists. Some returns give only numbers, but others give names and are therefore valuable to family historians. These records are usually in the diocesan record office (which is usually the same place as the local record office).

State records in the 16th and 17th centuries (particularly 1660–91)

Quarter sessions

These are by far the most important, and in many cases the only evidence of our ancestors' nonconformity. Until the Civil War the long lists of churchwardens' presentments for not coming to church consist either of Catholics or people who preferred to play bowls or drink.

During the Commonwealth period the Presbyterians continued to insist on everyone going to church, but this was a period of freedom (or anarchy, depending on your point of view) and they were not successful.

After the Restoration pressure on individuals to conform to Anglicanism was much greater. Yet more long lists of names were presented at quarter sessions, including individuals who are noted as 'quaker', 'anabaptist, 'sectary' or 'papist'. When religious identification is not given, further research is needed to place your ancestor with a particular group. The best clue is usually the name of the preacher at the offending meeting, or that of the owner of the meeting house. However, many groups were fluid and definitions may be impossible.

Where the facts were not clear, or where nonconformists wished to argue their case, magistrates had the option of tendering the Oath of Supremacy. This was unacceptable to nonconformists, but refusing to take the oath was a crime and nonconformists could be sent to prison until they were willing to swear. This was the technical reason why many nonconformists spent long periods in prison.

Many quarter sessions records are in print and likely to be found at the SoG and in the local record office or local studies library. Dissenters cease to appear in the records after 1688, when nonconformity was granted legal toleration.

Yet again, Quakers took positions which other dissenters did not take. They refused to serve in the militia or to pay for substitutes and might be cited before quarter sessions at any time in the 18th century for their refusal to do so.

State Papers Domestic (PRO)

The State Papers Domestic relate to every matter with which government was concerned and therefore contain a vast amount of material, which is not systematically arranged. The material itself is on microfilm on open access at Kew, but fortunately the papers are calendared (summarized) to 1704 and there are indexes to the calendars. Start by looking for references to 'puritans', 'dissenters' or 'nonconformists'; other references may be under the county or town or the name of the officer or commissioner making the report. There are many lists of those refusing to come to church, but reasons for refusal may not always be clear.

Many people who were known Puritans may not be referred to as such in every document regarding them; this is clearly true, for example, of Parliamentarian officers during the Civil War. The only answer is imaginative browsing.

The Protestation Oath of 1641 (PRO)

This was a declaration in favour of Protestantism in general and Puritans did not object to it. It was intended to identify Catholics, but in practice many Catholics appear to have signed.

State records from the Civil War and the Commonwealth (1642–60)

For most of this period the Anglican church lost its status as the national church. The Puritan groups are prominent in the records and a range of new religious groups flourished (most of them not for long): the best known were the Seekers, Ranters, Levellers, Millenarians, Fifth Monarchy Men, Muggletonians and Quakers. Of these, only the last two survived and only the Quakers were numerically important in the long term.

Most of these groups were not interested in setting up formal churches or keeping the basic baptism/marriage/burial records which aid family history research. However, there is a great deal of material about them, including many unsystematic lists of their adherents, in State Papers Domestic, quarter sessions, pamphlets, private correspondence and the special series of records set up at this period (all in the PRO). These are:

SP 16	State Papers Domestic: Charles I (includes Navy Committee)
SP 19	Committee for the Advance of Money
SP 20	Committee for Sequestration of Delinquents' Estates
SP 21	Committee of Both Kingdoms
SP 22	Committee for Plundered Ministers
SP 23	Committee for Compounding with Delinquents
SP 24	Committee and Commissioners for Indemnity
SP 28	Commonwealth Exchequer Papers (includes the County Committees)

Many of these relate to officials and often to defeated royalists, but everyone on the Parliamentarian side was a Puritan.

There are a number of other records relating to 17th-century Puritans and dissenters. These are all in the Public Record Office. Most relate to the Puritan gentry, or at least to people with money.

Recusant rolls (PRO, E 376 and 377)

These records were set up in 1592 as part of government's campaign against Catholics – but the Act of 1581, which required attendance at church, and provided for a fine of £20 per month for failing to comply, was applied to non-conformists after 1660.

Abstracts of the first four recusant rolls (1592–6) have also been published by the Catholic Record Society (vols

18, 57 and 61), and the introduction to vol. 57 by H. Bowler explains in detail how the records work. The records are in Latin, densely abbreviated, and are not a beginner's source. No work has been done to establish how many of the entries after 1660 relate to Protestants.

The Lord Treasurer's Remembrancer's memoranda rolls (PRO, E 368)

These include evidence of convicted recusants going through the formal procedure to conform to the Church of England. They are primarily of importance for Catholic research, but there may be some Puritans listed in the rolls.

Pipe Office: declared accounts 1500–1817 (PRO, E 351)

These include information on the revenues received from nonconformists who were fined for not attending church. They are valuable for the period 1662–84.

Pipe Office miscellaneous rolls (PRO, E 370)

The rolls include fines levied for illegal preaching during the reign of Charles II.

Excommunications (PRO, C 85 and C 207)

The Anglican church retained the power to excommunicate, and the records of this should be in diocesan sources. Details of those who had been excommunicated were returned to Chancery; the records are arranged by diocese. Most of the diocesan returns in C 85 end in the late 16th century, but those in C 207 continue to the 19th century; there is a card index on open access in the PRO. There are 17th-century returns for Cheshire 1663–8 and 1671–90 in CHES 38.

There are further proceedings, including writs for the arrest of obstinate individuals, in KB 27 (to 1701), KB 28 (1702–) and KB 29. Appeals went to the High Court of Delegates.

Association Oath rolls (PRO, C 213)

These are general lists of those expressing loyalty to the king, but they include some lists of stated nonconformist ministers and congregations. Quakers are often conspicuous in oath rolls by affirming instead of swearing. C 213/170B contains an affirmation by London Quakers in support of the Association Oath. C 213/170A, however, is a standard declaration signed explicitly by Baptist ministers in and around London.

Sacrament certificates
(PRO, C 224, C 214, E 195, KB 22, CHES 4)

The Corporation Act of 1661 laid down that nobody could be legally elected to any office of local government without evidence that he had taken the Anglican sacrament of communion within the previous year. This was succeeded by the Test Act of 1672, which laid down that everyone holding office or a place of trust under the crown must take the Oaths of Allegiance and Supremacy and present a sacrament certificate. Those living within 30 miles of London had to take the oaths in either the Court of Chancery or Court of King's Bench, and thus those records are held in the PRO. Those living outside this radius had to take the oaths at the quarter sessions. Many of the records continue until 1828.

This is negative evidence; nonconformists should not have taken the Oath of Supremacy so, in principle, if your ancestors are in these records they cannot have been nonconformists. A sacrament certificate may help to date their decision to join the Church of England, perhaps a sign of upward mobility.

Register of places of worship (PRO, RG 31)

The Toleration Act of 1689 both permitted and required 'Protestant dissenting congregations' to register their meeting places with the clerk of the peace in their county or with the appropriate bishop or archdeacon. In 1852 the law was amended to require certification to the Registrar

General. At the same time every clerk of the peace and every bishop's and archdeacon's registrar was required to draw up a return of all the places of meeting that had been certified to them since the beginning. This series is therefore in principle an easy way into the more extensive and detailed records in quarter sessions and diocesan records.

There are two full series, which ought in principle to contain different material. In many cases those for the dioceses do not go back to the beginning, but entries are likely to describe the meeting place, often a private house, in terms of who owned or occupied it, and to give the parish and the names of those certifying. There is space for the name of the denomination, but this is often omitted.

The information is valuable evidence as to how many meeting places were intended to be used, but there was no requirement to re-register, or to de-register, and it is therefore not possible to know how long, if at all, these meeting places were used. If only a reasonable proportion of them were used for a few years by separate congregations, then they are a reminder of what may be missing from the series of authenticated non-parochial registers in RG 4.

State records in the 18th and 19th centuries

During the 18th and 19th centuries dissenters (nonconformists) were legal and prosperous. They appear in most series of public records, but not on account of their religion. However, note that nonconformists are barely represented in the enormous record series relating to the 19th-century Army or Navy. They were not a group that fitted in with the aims and structures of the military.

The nonconformists' involvement in changing the system – and the records!

The nonconformists' exclusion from positions of power meant that they had concentrated their attention on business and trade. They benefited enormously from the Industrial Revolution and the shift of power from the country to the towns. They lobbied effectively for social reforms which weakened the power of the Anglican church and, incidentally, created many of the great family history records. After the Reform Act of 1832, which gave the vote to the middle classes, they were instrumental in obtaining:

- the reform of the Poor Laws (1834)

- the creation of registry offices for marriages and the establishment of registration of births, marriages and deaths (1837)

- the deposit of their own records (1840)

- the closure of Anglican cemeteries in towns and the opening of borough cemeteries with unconsecrated ground suitable for nonconformist burial (1853)

- a state system for proving wills (1858)

- a state system of education (1870)

In the meantime they grew in numbers and importance. By the time of the Ecclesiastical Census of 1851 (PRO, HO 129) over half of those who attended a place of worship went to a nonconformist chapel. This source is not as useful as it sounds. One form was filled out for each place of worship giving details of the numbers who attended the services on census Sunday. The only name is likely to be that of the minister.

The nonconformist influence after 1851 continued to be very important, and has not yet died out.

As has been noted, the prime records for nonconformist family history after 1837 are state ones, not religious ones. Nevertheless, church membership and minute books, Sunday school records, missionary records, newspapers, magazines and pamphlets and, above all, testimonies, spiritual biographies and obituaries provide a wealth of personal detail about the church life of ordinary nonconformists that can rarely be found for ordinary Anglicans.

> ### ⓘ Remember
>
> Before the Civil War began in 1642 there were almost no separate nonconformist congregations. From then until 1688 nonconformists were subject to legal pressure, but after that they had freedom of worship. The various nonconformist groups had a lot in common with each other and by the 19th century many people went to their choice of church or chapel without worrying too much about its official denominational label.
>
> There were many short-lived congregations which have left no formal records, but nonconformists were almost all respectable citizens and are likely to be found in records of births, marriages and deaths, the census, wills and other standard sources.

FURTHER READING

J. Besse, *Collection of the Sufferings of the People called Quakers* (1753). Facsimile reprint of Yorkshire (William Session, 1998) and Westmorland, Cumberland, Northumberland and Durham, Isle of Man and Lancashire (William Sessions, 1999).

G. R. Breed, *My Ancestors were Baptists,* 3rd edn (SoG, 1995).

D. J. H. Clifford, *My Ancestors were Congregationalists*, 2nd edn (SoG, 1997).

M. J. Gandy, *Basic facts about English Nonconformity for Family Historians* (Federation of Family History Societies, 1998).

Robin D. Gwynn, *Huguenot Heritage: The History and Contribution of the Huguenots in Britain* (Routledge, 1985).

W. Lamont, 'The Muggletonians 1652–1979', *Past and Present* 99, May 1983.

W. Leary, *My Ancestors were Methodists*, 3rd edn (SoG, 1999).

E. H. Milligan and M. J. Thomas, *My Ancestors were Quakers*, 3rd edn (SoG, 1999).

M. Mullett, *Sources for the History of English Nonconformity 1660–1830* (BRA, Archives and the User no. 8, 1991).

A. Ruston, *My Ancestors were English Presbyterians/ Unitarians* (SoG, 1993).

D. Shorney, *Protestant Nonconformity and Roman Catholicism* (PRO, 1996).

D. J. Steel, *Sources for Nonconformist Genealogy and Family History*, National Index of Parish Registers vol. 2 (SoG, 1973).

R. Wiggins, *My Ancestors were in the Salvation Army* (SoG, 1997).